Miniatures

• 8 Original Piano Solos •

By William Gillock

CONTENTS

These solos were originally in the series *Piano–All the Way!*

ISBN 978-1-5400-2560-9

EXCLUSIVELY DISTRIBUTED BY

Visit Hal Leonard Online at
www.halleonard.com

Contact us:
Hal Leonard
7777 West Bluemound Road
Milwaukee, WI 53213
Email: info@halleonard.com

In Europe, contact:
Hal Leonard Europe Limited
42 Wigmore Street
Marylebone, London, W1U 2RN
Email: info@halleonardeurope.com

In Australia, contact:
Hal Leonard Australia Pty. Ltd.
4 Lentara Court
Cheltenham, Victoria, 3192 Australia
Email: info@halleonard.com.au

Birthday Party*

Waltz tempo

William Gillock

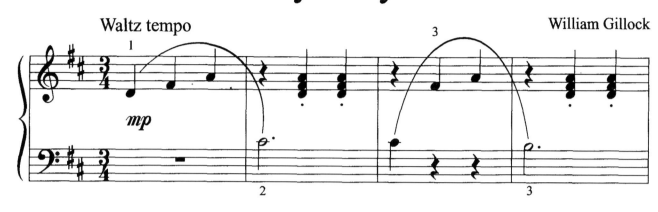

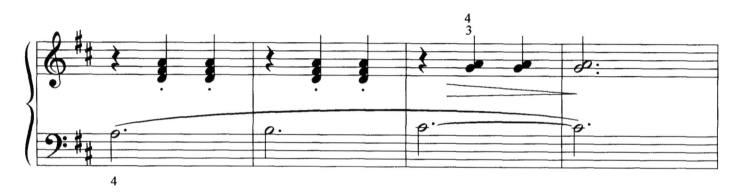

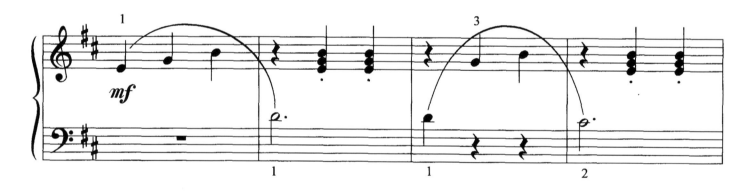

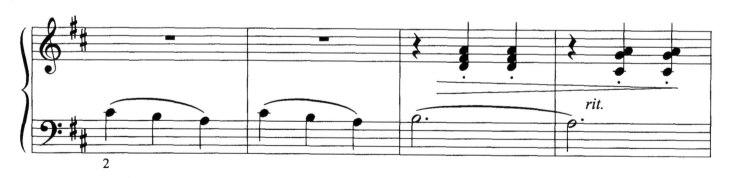

* Original key: D-flat major

From *Piano--All the Way!*, Level Two

On Rollerblades

William Gillock

Allegretto

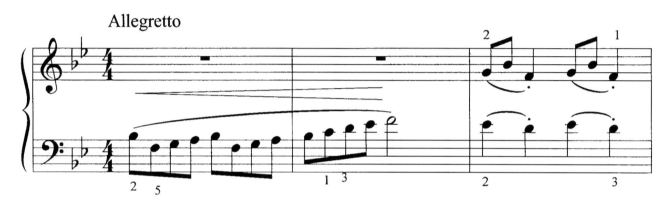

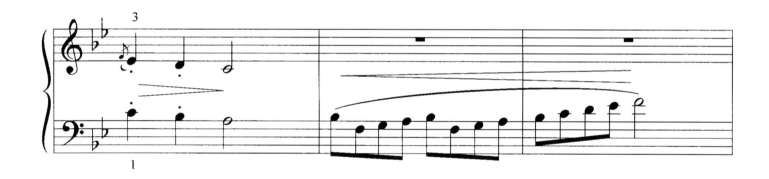

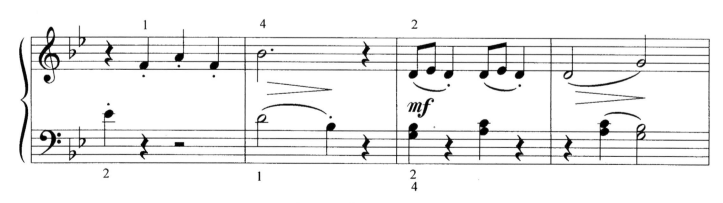

From *Piano--All the Way!*, Level Three
© MCMLXIX by The Willis Music Co.

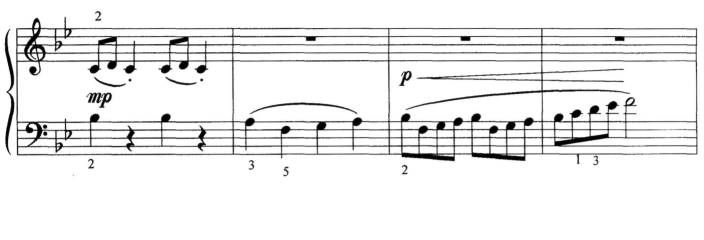

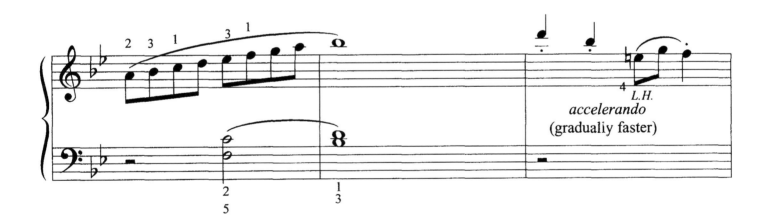

The Harpist

William Gillock

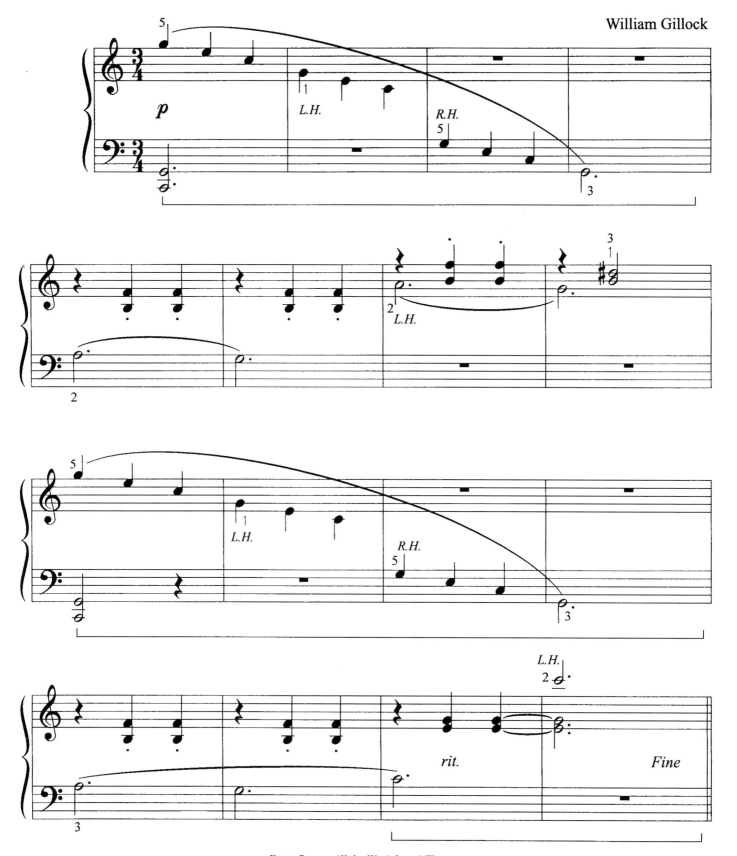

From *Piano--All the Way!*, Level Three
© MCMLXIX by The Willis Music Co.

7

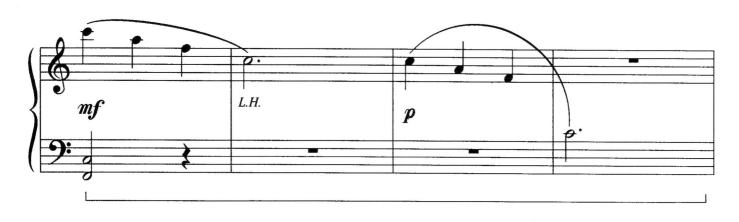

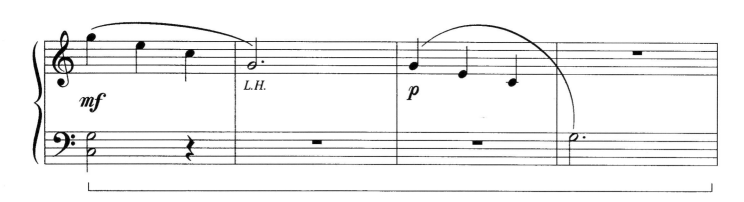

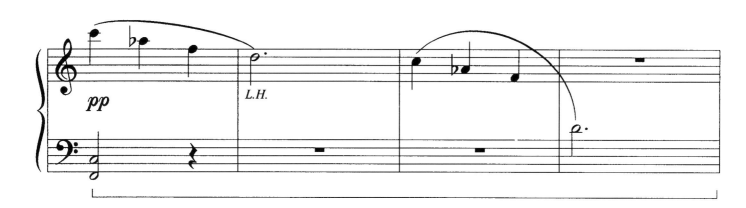

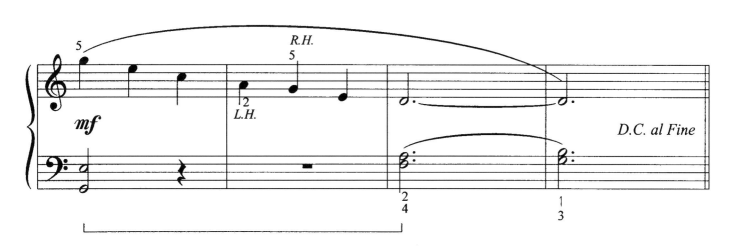

Allegro in G

William Gillock

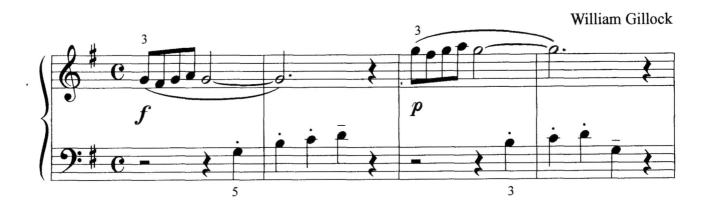

From *Piano--All the Way!*, Level Three
© MCMLXIX by The Willis Music Co.

A Graceful Waltz

William Gillock

From *Piano--All the Way!*, Level Two
© MCMLXIX by The Willis Music Co.

Riding the Range*

William Gillock

*Original key: A major

From *Piano--All the Way!*, Level Three
© MCMLXIX by The Willis Music Co.

Bells Across the Lagoon*

Adagio (**con poco moto)

William Gillock

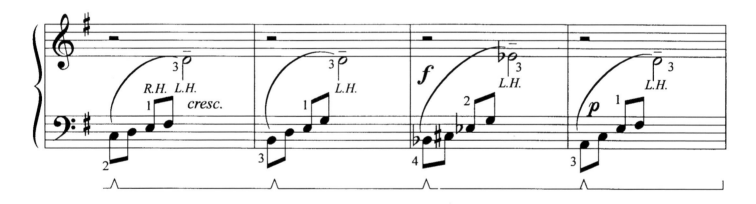

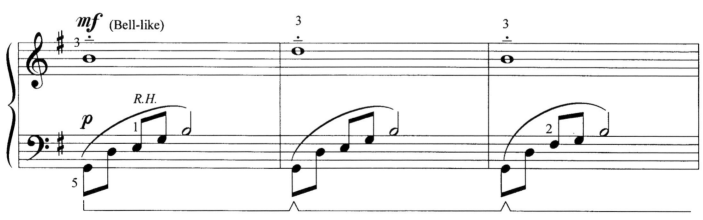

*Original key: A-flat major
** with a little motion

From *Piano--All the Way!*, Level Three
© MCMLXIX by The Willis Music Co.

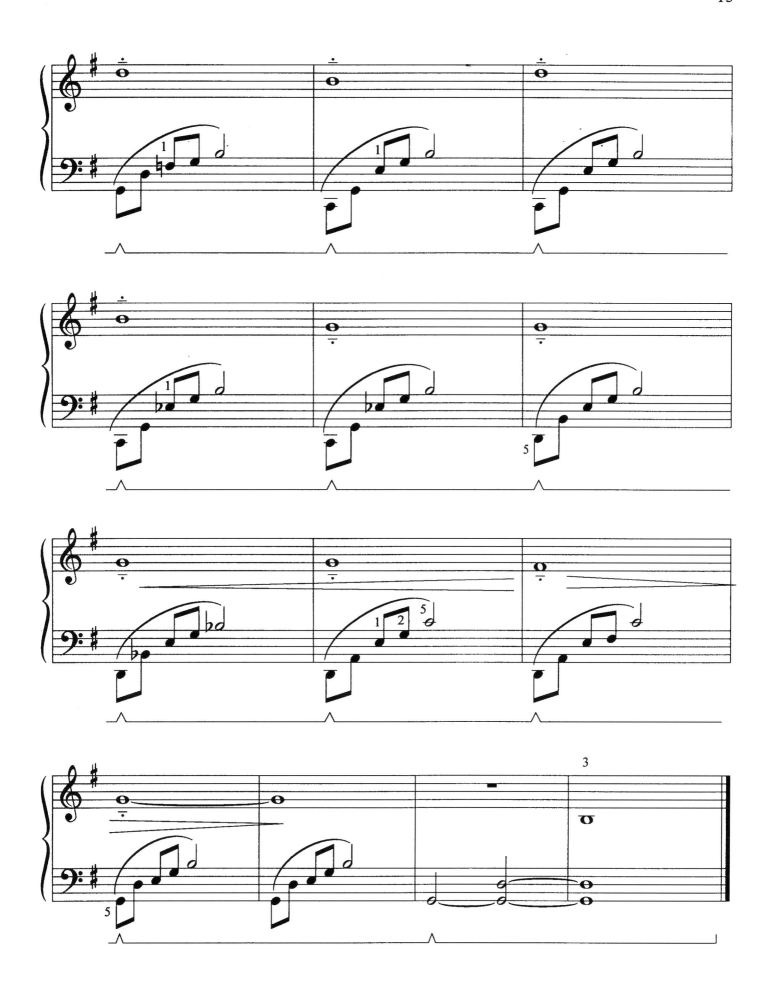

Spooky Night

William Gillock

From *Piano--All the Way!*, Level Two
© MCMLXIX by The Willis Music Co.